REPTILE
COLORING BOOK
FOR ADULTS

AN ADULT COLORING BOOK OF 40 REPTILES INCLUDING SNAKES, LIZARDS, TURTLES AND MORE IN A VARIETY OF PATTERNS

ADULT COLORING WORLD

ISBN-13: 978-1522797463

ISBN-10: 1522797467

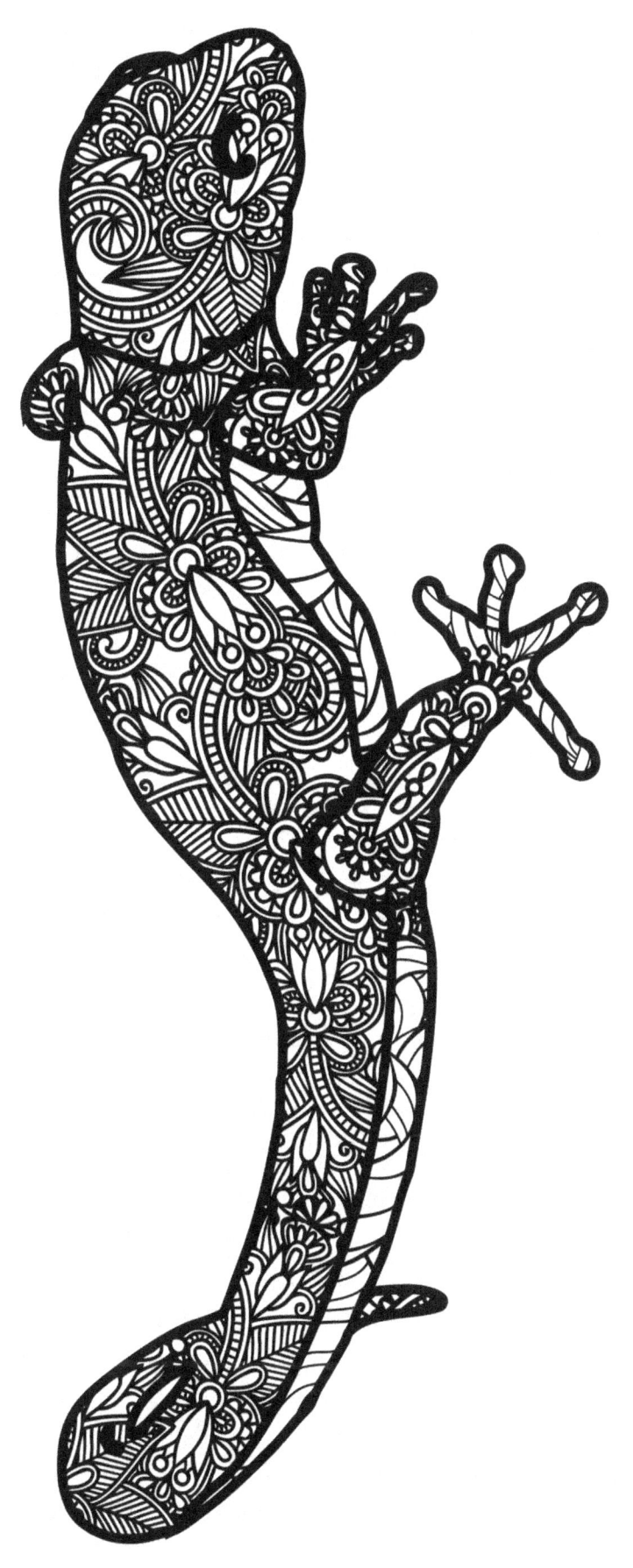

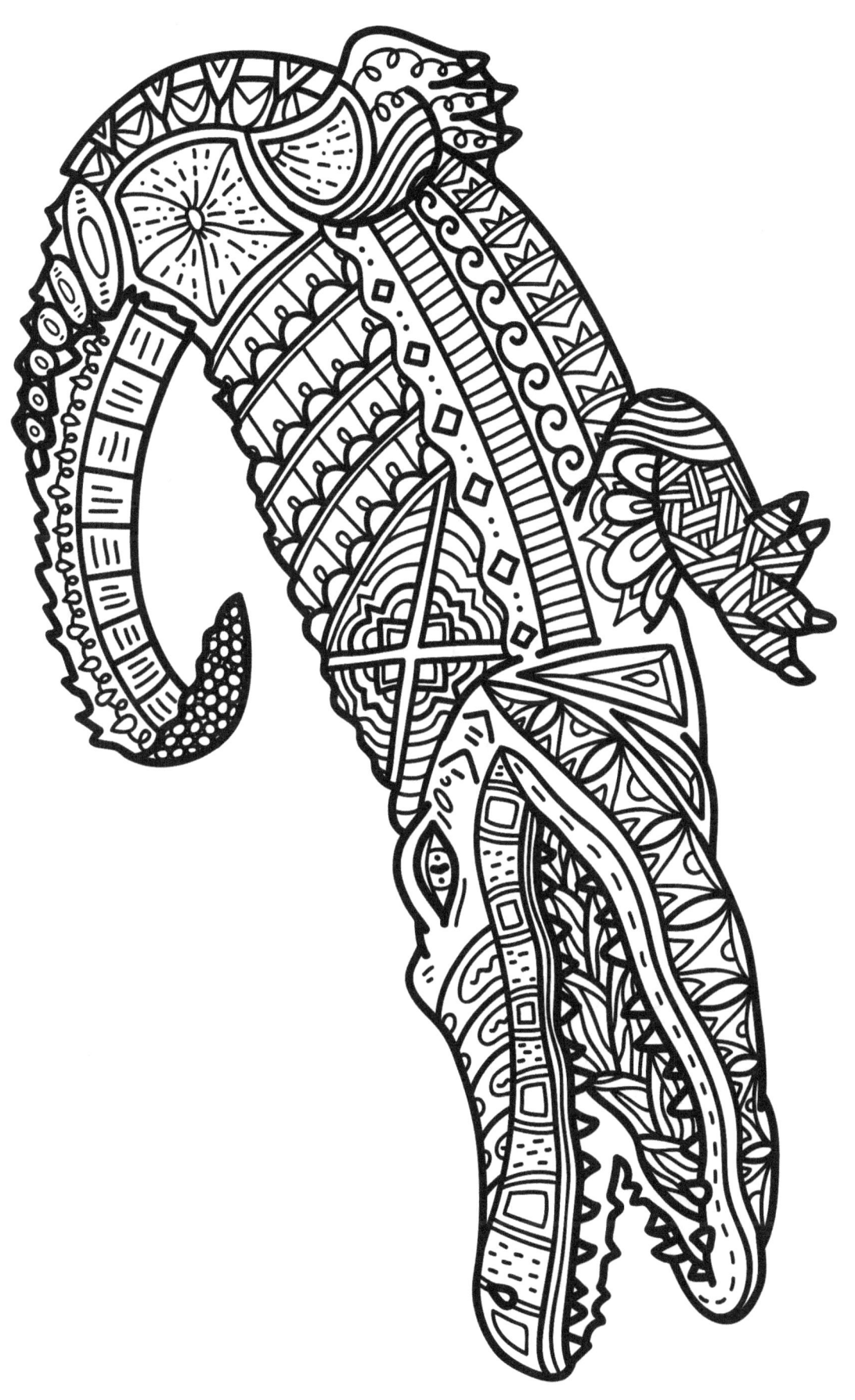

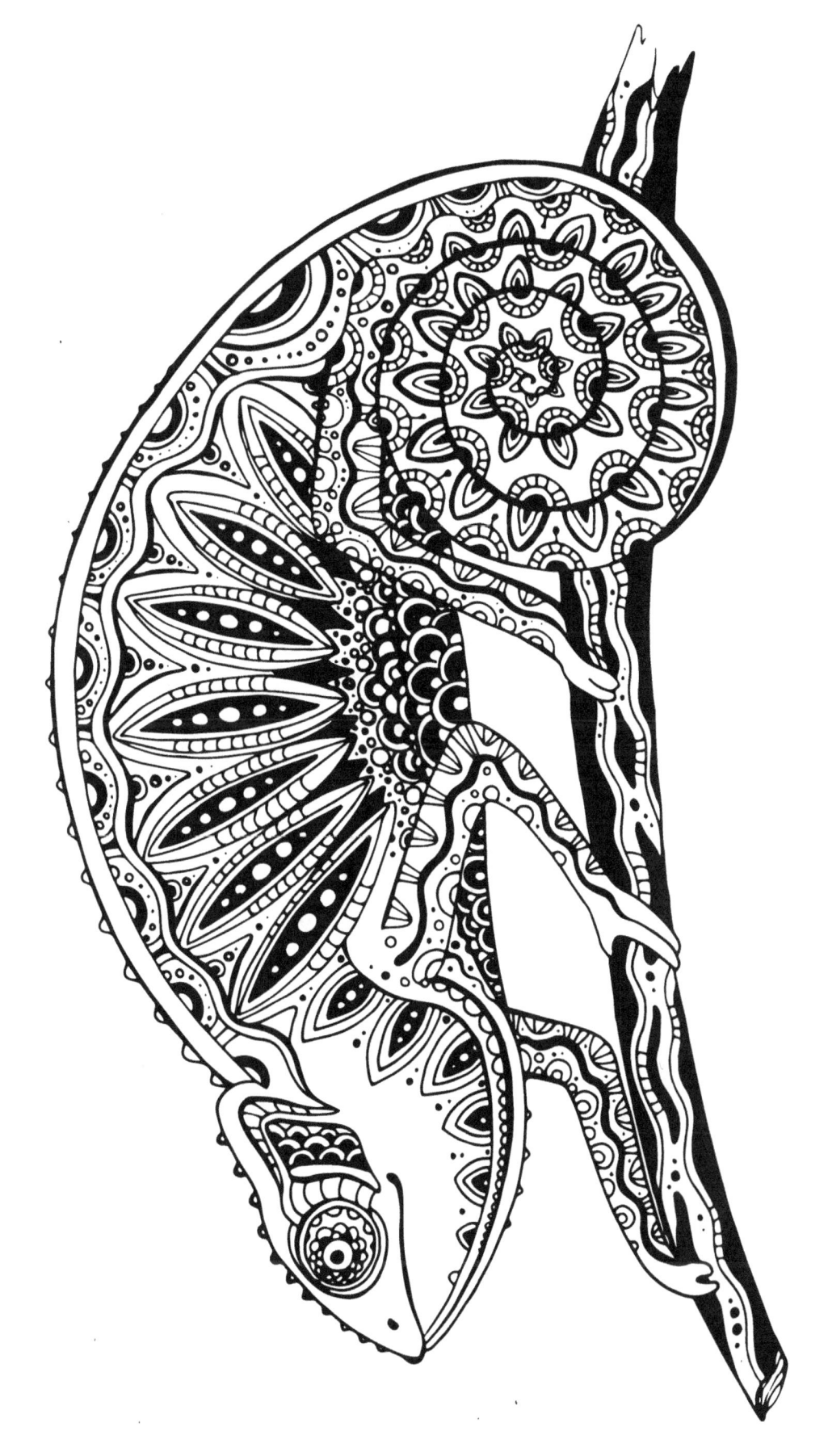

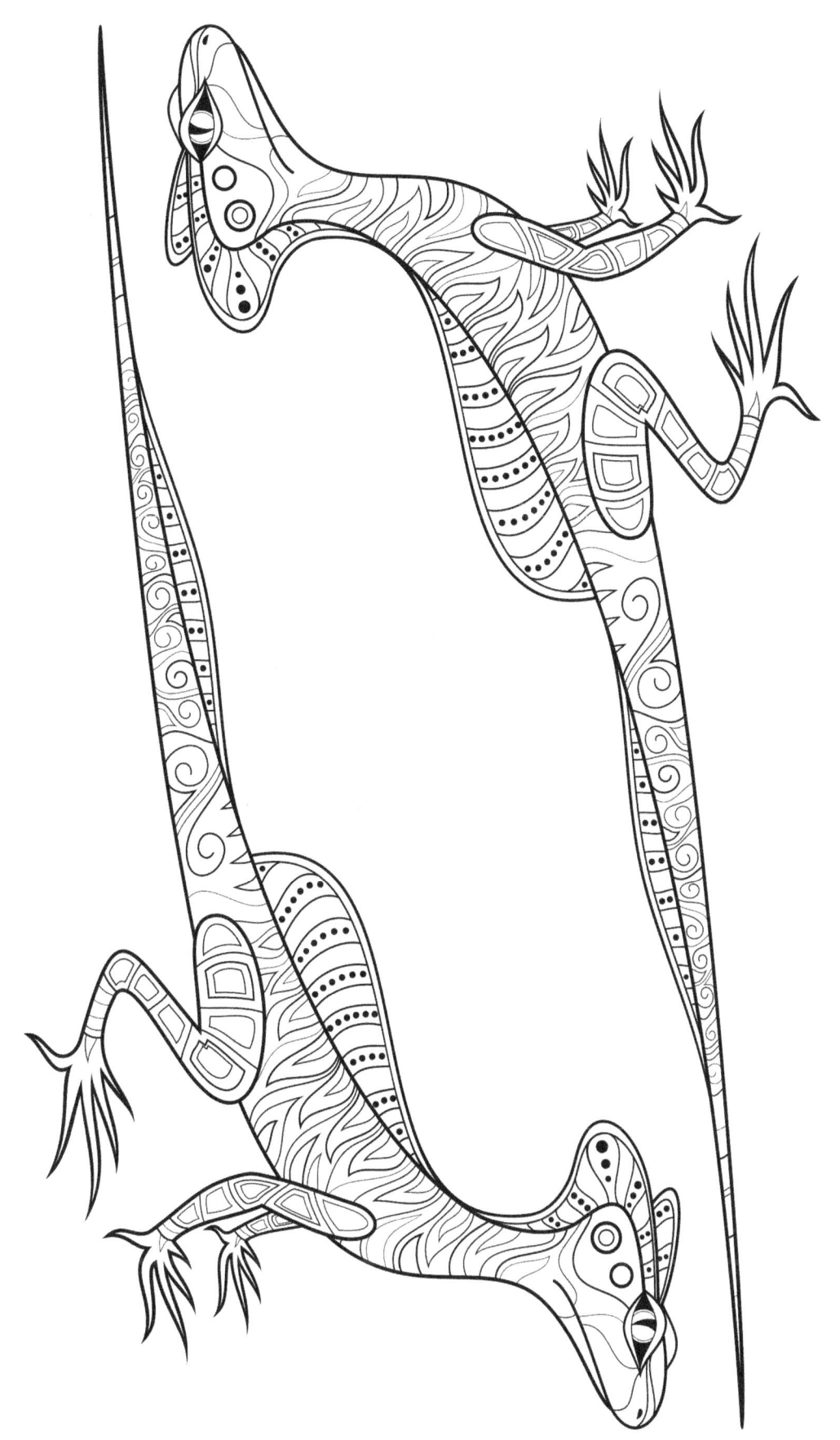

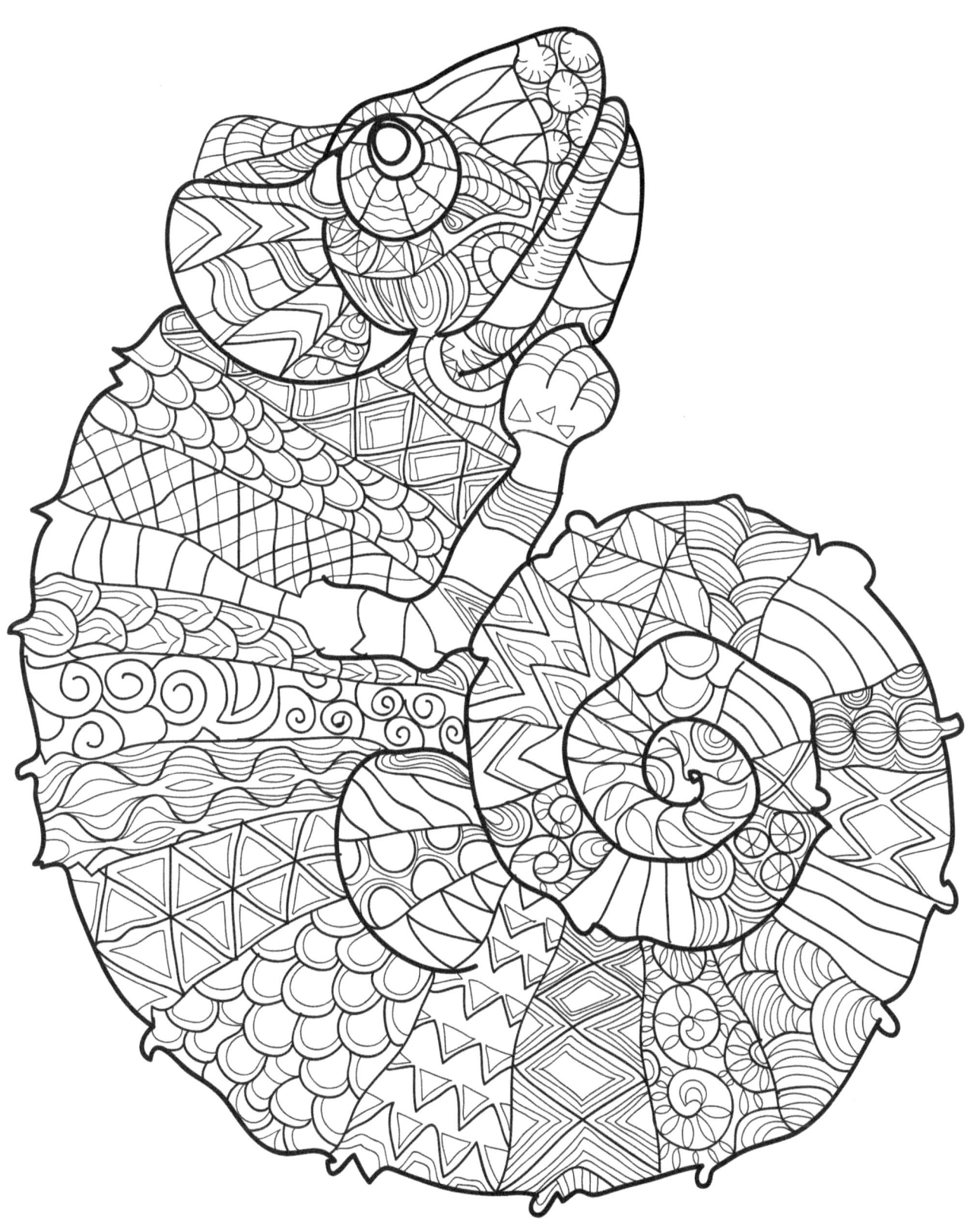

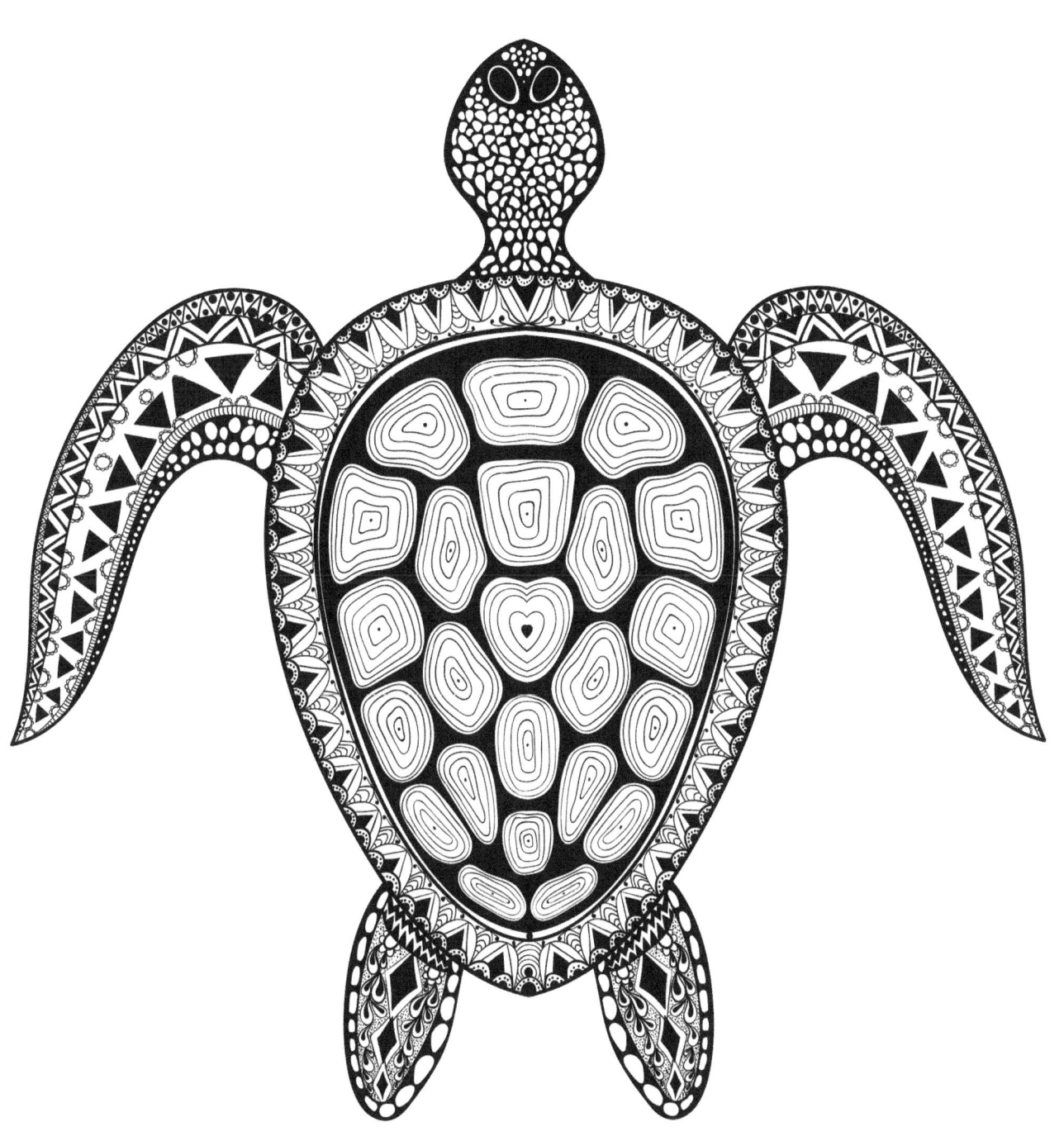

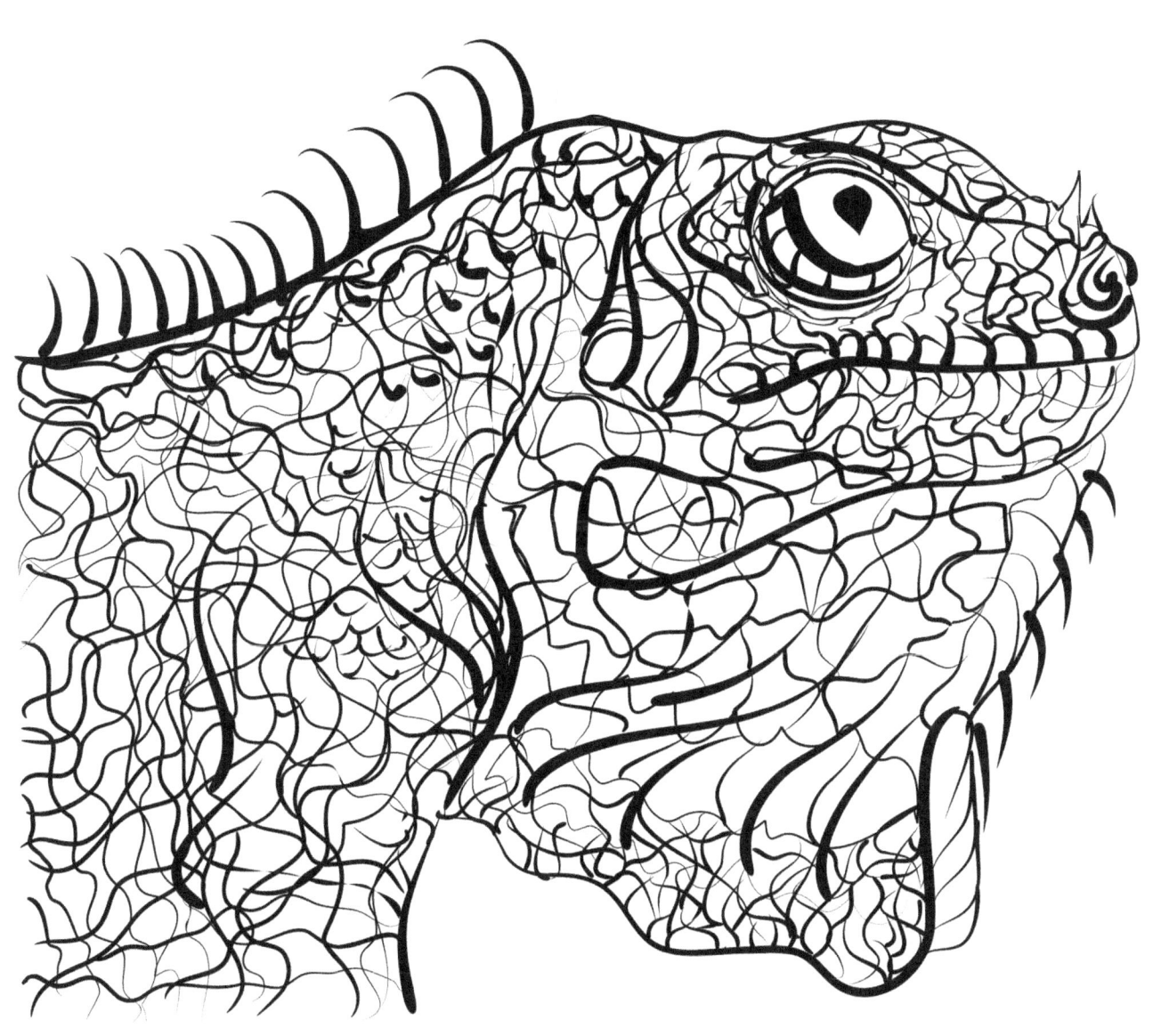

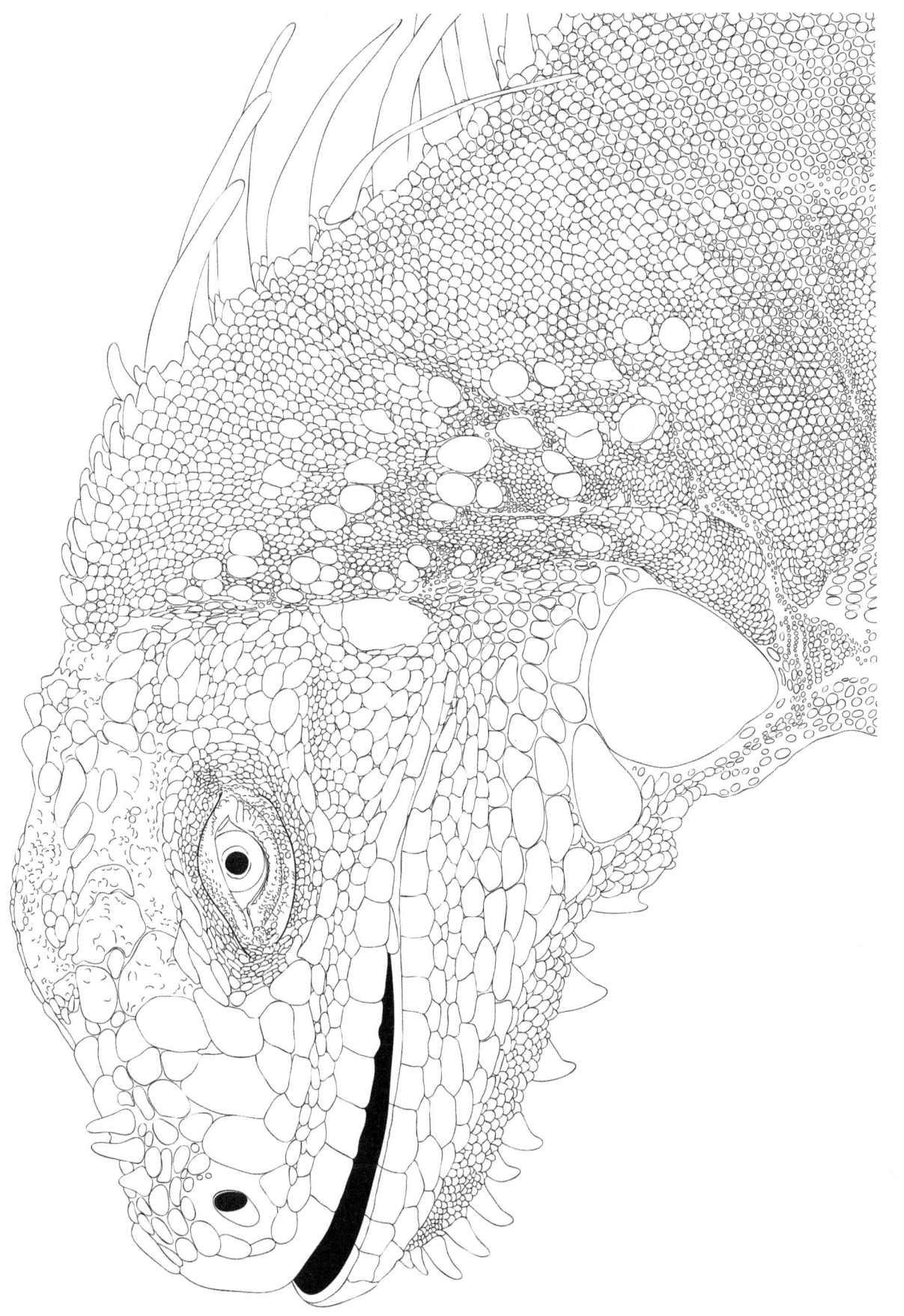

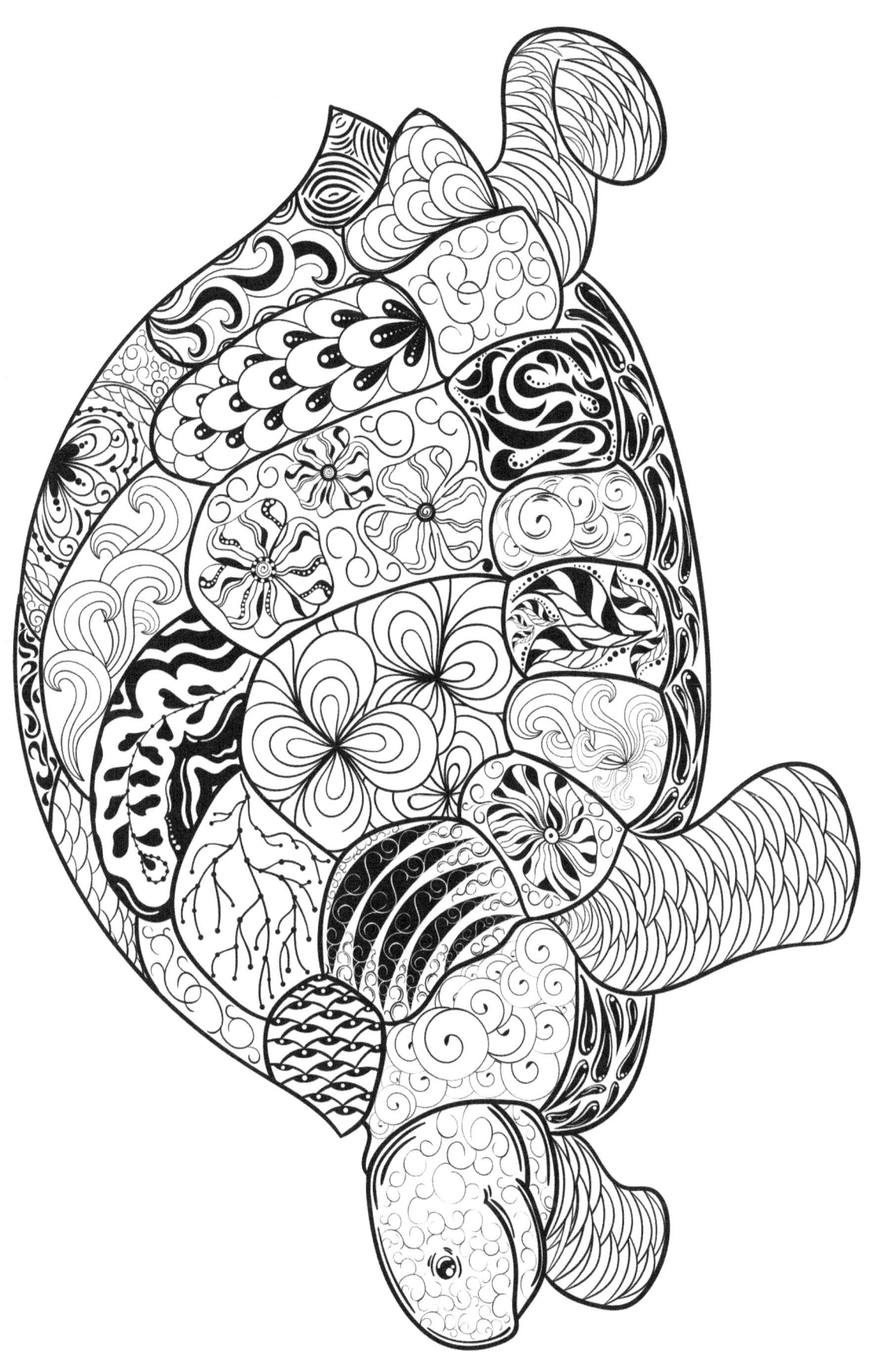

www.ingramcontent.com/pod-product-compliance
Lightning Source LLC
Chambersburg PA
CBHW081236280526
45787CB00006B/2673